Twin Flame Ascension™
Take Me Home Oracle Deck

By Dr. Harmony
Artwork by Tatiana Hassan

Copyright © 2021 U.S. GAMES SYSTEMS, INC.
All rights reserved. The illustrations, cover design, and contents are protected by copyright. No part of this book may be reproduced in any form without permission in writing from the publisher, except by a reviewer who wishes to quote brief passages in connection with a review written for inclusion in a magazine, newspaper or website.

10 9 8 7 6 5 4 3

Made in China

Published by
U.S. GAMES SYSTEMS, INC.
179 Ludlow Street
Stamford, CT 06902 USA
www.usgamesinc.com

TABLE OF CONTENTS

Introduction	7
Objective of the Deck	9
About the Deck	11
How to Use the Deck	13
The Spreads	17
The Cards	26
Suit 1: Slate—11 Powerful Life Lessons That Will Expedite Your Ascension Process	26
Acknowledge	26
Divine Order	27
Awareness	28
Trust	30
Reprogram Your Soul	31
Beyond Illusion	33
Heal Abandonment	34
Speak Your Truth	35
Open Your Heart	37
Practice Self-Love	38
I Am Enough	39

Suit 2: Aqua—11 Steps in the Take Me Home
   Ascension Pathway 41
Surrender 41
Spiritual Awakening 42
Increase Your Frequency 43
Transformation 45
Breakthrough 46
Integration 47
Rebirth 49
One with Self 50
Harmonize 51
Enter Your Vortex 53
Mission Accomplished 54
Suit 3: Red—11 Principles to Come Into Alignment
   with Yourself and Find True Love 56
The Chosen One 56
Remember Your Identity 57
Soul Merger 59
The Generator 60
The Electric 61
Karmic Purge 63
Healing Separation 64

Path of Least Resistance	65
Unification	67
Reunion	68
Take Me Home	69
Suit 4: Olive—11 Courtships That Will Facilitate Your Soul's Expansion	71
Karmic Relationship	71
False Twin Flame	72
Soulmate	73
Twin Flame Facilitator	75
Masculine Twin	76
Feminine Twin	78
King	79
Queen	81
High Priest	82
High Priestess	83
Twin Flame	85
Suit 5: Amber—11 Activation Codes That Will Accelerate Your Ascension	87
Clear Energy Blocks	87
Voyager's Journey	88
Merkaba Activation	89

Holy Grail Code	91
Master Alchemist	92
Clearing Karma	93
Mystical Messages	95
Honor Your Agreement	96
Sacred Sexuality	97
Divine Creativity	99
Compassion	100
About the Author	102
About the Artist	104

INTRODUCTION

WELCOME TO THE TWIN FLAME ASCENSION™—TAKE ME HOME ORACLE DECK

Twin flame ascension is a never-ending self-actualization process that begins when your inner soul-self becomes activated through a spiritual awakening. Remembering your identity takes place on or around the time you come into physical connection with your twin flame—the other half of you. This divine appointment occurs so that they can become your mirrored reflection to help you find real self-love and align with your life purpose. Your twin flame is your greatest teacher and their primary role is to assist you with finding your way home to inner peace and happiness.

The Take Me Home Pathway consists of 11

steps in the twin flame ascension journey. It is a rebirthing process that begins the moment you move beyond the illusion of being a hostage to extensive life challenges. This forces you to change your perception and embrace more fulfillment in all areas of life. I created this Twin Flame Ascension™—Take Me Home Oracle Deck as a tool to help you understand more about your personal process, as you shift from fear to freedom. This deck will help you gain new insight and higher wisdom, providing greater clarity about your twin flame journey.

Loads of Love and Light,

Dr. Harmony

OBJECTIVE OF THE DECK

The Twin Flame Ascension™—Take Me Home Oracle Deck is structured similarly to tarot cards. Just like the tarot concept, the ascension process takes you inward on a quest to accomplish major life lessons for personal growth that assist your soul's evolution. These lessons include completing soul contracts with others who become your teachers. They create challenging relationships and "mirrored reflections" that enable you to see your true self. Your twin flame is your greatest teacher with the strongest mirrored reflection. The twin flame ascension pathway teaches you how to transcend from "the Fool" and become "the Star" so you can share your light with the world.

This oracle deck is not about fortune telling. It was designed to help unlock your hidden power, discover who you are, elevate your soul's frequency, and become your true self so that you can live your best life. The intention of this deck is to help you align with your authentic truth, while balancing your inner masculine and inner feminine energies to create oneness with your divine source energy. When you align with your highest truth and heal your heart it brings balance within your inner soul self to have meaningful relationships and attract abundance in all areas of your life.

ABOUT THE DECK

The deck comprises 55 cards, which are divided into five color suits. Each color suit contains 11 cards—11:11 "Key Objectives" for you to master. Whether you have accomplished these concepts, you are in the process of accomplishing them, or you need more work to complete an area, each suit contains a path of transcendence that will help you release your past, raise your vibration, and reclaim your life from a higher perspective.

Numerological Sequence Meaning of Each Suit

- 1:1 – Balance between your inner masculine and feminine energies
- 2:2 – Balance within your inner-soul self
- 3:3 – Alignment with your higher self
- 4:4 – Alignment with your guides
- 5:5 – Alignment with your destiny

6:6 – Alignment with your inner masculine
7:7 – Alignment with your highest path
8:8 – Alignment with infinite potential
9:9 – Alignment with your inner feminine
10:10 – Alignment with Source energy
11:11 – Alignment with your beloved

The Energy of the Deck

Each image within this deck of cards is encoded with mandalas. A mandala (from the Sanskrit language) is a circular symbol that represents the cosmos and universe. It is derived from sacred geometric shapes. Each pattern determines a frequency of energy that is emitted from each of the images.

HOW TO USE THE DECK

Prepare and Charge Your Cards

Place your cards face up in the sunlight for a period of two or three hours, or lay the deck in a windowsill overnight to absorb the moonlight energy. In addition, you can also place a clear quartz or selenite crystal on top of the deck, as it charges in the light. Smudging with white sage is also sufficient.

One of the most powerful ways to charge your deck of cards with your personal vibration is to hold the cards in your right hand—face down, while placing your left hand over your heart chakra. Close your eyes and connect to the presence of your energy, while speaking intentional words from your heart, or you can repeat the following prayer:

"Dear Archangel Michael and Spirit Guides, I

ask that you assist me with the purification of this oracle card deck. I ask that you reveal to me the purest and clearest awareness that serves my highest good. Please fill this deck of cards with your presence of diamond white light—the color of God's love—rainbow light. Surround this deck with high vibrational peace and protection every time I use it. I ask to be shielded and protected from any lower vibrational frequencies and ask that this deck only deliver guidance from a frequency of love or above."

And, So It Is!

Shuffle the Deck and Set Your Intention

You can effectively set your intention by placing the deck of cards in your left hand—face down and with your right hand or fist tap the top of the deck five times. Center yourself by getting present. Open your mind and align with your heart space. Then, make a connection with your higher self and invite in your angelic guides of the highest love and light to assist you with clarity to provide direction with inner peace and comfort.

It is very powerful to set your intention and ask for guidance while shuffling the cards. While doing so, pay attention to your thoughts, feelings, emotions, and any visions that may come to your awareness. You may ask a simple question that you seek guidance and direction for but it is best to refrain from "yes" or "no" questions. Trust yourself and what you are feeling. Know that the signs, signals, and wisdom that you are receiving are from the highest love and light and are delivered from your higher self and your higher guidance. Stay heart centered and choose the cards that resonate with your intuition. Notice any cards that stick out, clump together, or fall out. This is a sign that those cards are relevant to your questions. The main thing is that you follow and honor your instinct. There is no right or wrong way to shuffle the deck. After asking your question, allow your intuition to direct you so you can proceed with one or more of the following spreads.

THE SPREADS

The Pyramid Spread

This spread is designed to help you gain solutions for a particular situation that is currently showing up in your life.

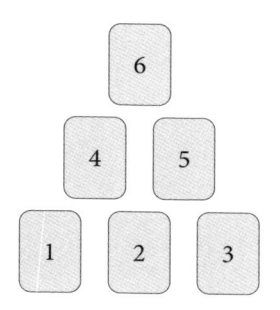

```
        [6]
     [4]   [5]
   [1]  [2]  [3]
```

Row 1: What is your present situation?
Card 1 – Past Lesson
Card 2 – Present Area of Focus
Card 3 – Future Resolution

Row 2: What action do you need to take?
Card 4 – Brings Balance to Your Inner Self
Card 5 – Helps You Move Forward Faster

Row 3: Potential responses
Card 6 – Possible Solutions/Outcomes

The 11 = 11 Spread

This spread is designed to reveal your personal blocks and how they pertain to the mirrored reflection of your twin flame so you can see what is pulling you out of alignment. It will also direct you towards taking appropriate actions to harmonize your inner status, bringing balance within your inner masculine and inner feminine energies.

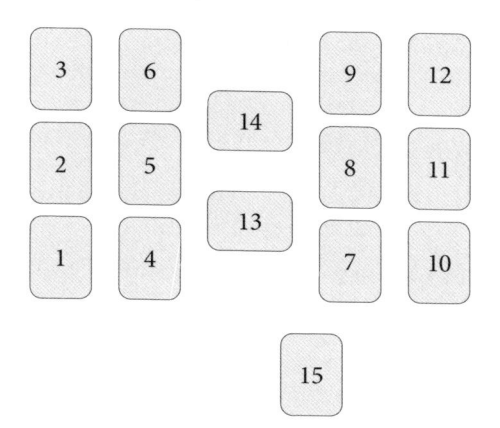

Column 1: Your Inner Feminine

Card 1 – Overview of your divine feminine energy

Card 2 – What aspect of your inner feminine is blocked?

Card 3 – What action is needed to overcome this obstacle?

Column 2: Your Inner Masculine
Card 4 – Overview of your divine masculine energy
Card 5 – What aspect of your inner masculine is blocked?
Card 6 – What action is needed to take to overcome this obstacle?

Column 3: Integration of the Divine Feminine and Divine Masculine
Card 13 – What obstacle is blocking you from aligning with your beloved?
Card 14 – What action do you need to take to overcome this obstacle?

Column 4: Your Mirrored Reflection From Your Beloved's Inner Feminine
Card 7 – What is your beloved teaching you to let go of that would support your inner feminine growth?
Card 8 – What obstacle is preventing you from expressing yourself?

Card 9 – What is blocking you from connecting with your inner goddess?

Column 5: Your Mirrored Reflection From Your Beloved's Inner Masculine

Card 10 – What is your beloved teaching you to let go of that would support your inner masculine growth?

Card 11 – What obstacle is preventing you from stepping into personal empowerment?

Card 12 – What is blocking you from connecting with your inner warrior?

Bottom of the Deck:

Card 15 – Potential outcome for physical merger with your beloved

The Take Me Home Pathway—11 Steps to Finding True Love!

This spread will take you on an inward quest to unlock your hidden power so you can discover who you truly are. This enlightenment process helps you transcend your shadows and align with your greatest potential. Depending on your personal situation, each card reveals if the task is already accomplished (past), if you are working to accomplish it (present), or if it needs to be accomplished (future).

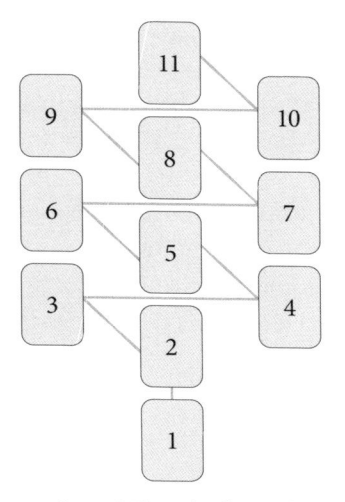

Step 1: Surrender – What shadows do you need to release?

Step 2: Spiritual Awakening – What action steps are required to change your situation?

Step 3: Raise Your Frequency – What hidden truths should be brought to your awareness to enable a higher perspective?

Step 4: Transformation – What perceptions need to change?

Step 5: Breakthrough – Where do you need to focus to keep moving forward?

Step 6: Integration – What information do you need to process more thoroughly to gain greater clarity?

Step 7: Rebirth – Look deeper within. What do you still need to release to rise above your situation?

Step 8: One with Self – What do you need to work on to bring balance within?

Step 9: Harmonize – Where do you need to place your attention that would allow your light to shine brighter?

Step 10: Enter Your Vortex – What areas in your life are coming into alignment?

Step 11: Mission Accomplished – What will bring you joy, happiness, and inner peace?

THE CARDS

Slate – 11 Powerful Life Lessons that Will Expedite Your Ascension Process

1:1 Acknowledge– Take Responsibility

Taking responsibility for your actions gives you the momentum to create your own reality. When you come to terms with what no longer works in your life and realize that your current status is an accumulation of previous choices, you will recognize how inner feelings impact your life. The first step towards owning your truth is to acknowledge that you carry the power within you to make positive life decisions that align with your heart's desires.

This card implies that you are the "key holder" of your destiny and no one except you can unlock your hidden potential. If you are unhappy with yourself, your life, your relationships, or even your career, only you can take necessary actions that will shift your situation—making you the alchemist of your reality.

You are being called to rise above limitations that have caused you to focus on what is outside of yourself, which creates separation between you and all that is. Making this conscious connection with your inner-soul flame will set your soul on fire and light on your path—resulting in a brighter future.

2:2 Divine Order– Practice Patience

Patience is the ultimate virtue. You are experiencing many challenges that teach you tolerance, trust, and timing; all requiring you to practice patience— a major life lesson that you must master for your soul to evolve. This card suggests that you release control and allow divine guidance to direct you, which demonstrates that you trust the process.

Practicing patience will enhance your ability to connect with your senses and teach you to let go of the idea that you are the only one who can achieve what you perceive as perfect or the right way. This card implies that you need to get out of your own way by releasing logical concepts and surrender control, creating space for you to receive blessings that will far exceed the expectations of your mind.

Rushing the process will cause you to make hasty decisions. This diminishes your ability to create at your highest capacity. Make a commitment to exercise self-control, which will enhance your ability to live more consciously in the present moment so you can attract your greatest potential.

3:3 Awareness–
Crystal Clear Vision

Developing conscious awareness starts with your ability to tune inward and integrate the state of your mind, body, heart and soul, which provides introspective consciousness in regards to your "YOU-niverse" and how it aligns with your physical reality. This requires that you are present, which enables you to see everything from a higher perspective.

This card indicates that you need to take inventory of your internal and external surroundings. Pay particular attention to your thoughts, feelings, actions, and how you view your world. Use your expanded awareness to help you rise above logical limitations and tap into your own creative abilities that will bring your desires into form.

Viewing your life from a heightened state generates power in your present moment so that your soul can evolve further and faster. Crystal-clear vision eliminates confusion that has blocked your ability to move forward with confidence in the direction of your soul path. If you stay consistent, your accumulated efforts will create exponential growth that will lead you towards infinite possibilities.

4:4 Trust–
Ask · Listen · Allow

You are a bright light with innate intelligence that lies deep within your soul. This card is reminding you to trust this celestial wisdom. Your higher mind is in control of your every heartbeat. Without conscious thought it orchestrates the waves of your breath that harmonically flow in and out.

This card suggests that you make the intentional effort to trust yourself and your journey. Ask for guidance, listen for solutions, and allow the process to unfold. This will help you let go of fear and stop worrying, waiting, or wondering about your future, which pulls you out of alignment with your heart.

Lack of trust blocks you from going forward on your divine path. Over time, the more you trust, the more you can release. This is an unfolding process that will help you attain greater awareness. Making a conscious effort to let your higher intelligence handle your challenges helps you develop trust and makes your journey a more enjoyable experience.

5:5 Reprogram Your Soul–
Release · Raise · Reclaim

Your higher guidance suggests you release all that no longer serves your greater good in life, love, and livelihood! Your soul is programmed with negative memories from every experience you have encountered in all times, spaces, and realities throughout your soul's evolutionary journey. These imprints have created stories that are deep seated within your soul and are still controlling your actions.

This card suggests you reprogram your soul by releasing attachments to people, places, and things that are not supporting you. This action will raise your energetic frequency, leaving your heart free to align with your highest potential. Cutting ties to these barriers removes interference in your soul's frequency, which has blocked you from tuning into your highest vibration.

Bringing your energy into balance restores heart wholeness and ignites your inner-soul flame. This sense of being complete will enhance your ability to experience love in all areas of your life. You will not only radiate love for everything you do going forward, but you find appreciation and gratitude for all that is allowing you to reclaim your life in this higher state of being.

6:6 Beyond Illusion–
Change Your Perception

Move beyond your limitations and view your journey through the lens of your heart. Your thoughts, feelings and beliefs send signals into the universe in relation to the frequency of your emotional state. Through changing your perception, you can bypass challenging situations. This accelerates your ascension because everything starts to match your higher frequency.

Shifting your focus beyond the illusion of perceived obstacles releases unnecessary struggles, making it easier to let go of old stories, past programming, or belief systems that belong to others. When you face fears with a positive perception it attracts your greater good, which is helping you create a new reality in this higher state of being.

This card serves as a reminder that when you are

in alignment with your infinite potential, it brings balance to the finite thoughts that have pulled you out of neutrality with your Source energy. As your soul expands and your perspective elevates, it creates an opportunity for you to discover more about yourself.

7:7 Heal Abandonment– Time to Forgive

You have experienced abandonment in multiple lifetimes. Wounded stories are subconsciously causing you intense soul pain that makes you easily triggered when you experience rejection or unrequited love. This card implies that you need to heal traumatic experiences and the influence of unhealthy relationships.

You have been abandoning your own needs, which is the same as not loving yourself. You will move beyond the fear of abandonment when you realize that you caused yourself this pain because you've separated from yourself. It is time to forgive yourself for not standing up, showing up, or speaking up for your need to be heard, loved, or respected by others.

You were taught that to experience love, you must earn the love you seek. This produces the need for approval and creates feelings of rejection and feeling left out or left behind, causing you to justify your actions. Letting go of your old identity is painful because you experience the death of your former self and patterns. Yet it is necessary for you to create space for your new identity.

8:8 Speak Your Truth– Express Yourself

There is power in your ability to voice your truth! Before you can speak your truth you must first know your truth internally. Your truth is revealed through a process of learning to know who you are, identifying your core values, acknowledging your abilities, and awakening to what you came here to do.

Developing a relationship with yourself requires deep internal exploration to identify your patterns of thought, feelings and actions. The deeper connection you have with yourself—the more open, raw, and real you can become, which creates freedom. This inward journey enhances your ability to stand in your truth and express yourself from your heart. When you believe in who you are and what you represent, you begin to share a more authentic version of yourself.

This card suggests that you practice expressing yourself without fear of limitations or judgment. Make a conscious effort to accept who you are. Practice speaking your truth without worrying if you are going to hurt someone's feelings. This will help break patterns of pleasing others and honor yourself by saying "no" and setting loving boundaries.

9:9 Open Your Heart– Set Loving Boundaries

It is human nature to guard and protect yourself from being hurt again, but if you carry past pain with you, you will continue to put up a wall that prevents you from experiencing great love. Letting go of the fear of being hurt and setting loving boundaries teaches you to trust the process and open your heart to receive love.

This card indicates that you need to let go of your stories and cut energetic cords that are attached to judgment, expectations, and comparison to others. You may also be placing conditions on those around you by expecting them to fill a void that you need to fill from within. Be willing to forgive others who have hurt you. Learn to say "no" and set loving boundaries.

The more heart aligned you are, the greater is your ability to express yourself from the heart.

Giving your heart a voice allows you to attract abundance and to create a life you love. When you feel loved you show up as love and freely share love with the world.

10:10 Practice Self-Love–Nurture Your Inner Child

Self-love is a prerequisite for a heart-centered life. If you want the ultimate relationship, it starts with the relationship you have with yourself. Practicing self-love impacts your thoughts, feelings, emotions, your choices and actions, and your relationships.

The ability to love yourself is a direct reflection of how you perceive who you are in everyday life. You have experienced feelings of being unloved in many lifetimes that has left your inner child feeling neglected, causing you to feel separated from your inner source of love. When you feel hurt and rejected it causes your heart to close off, most likely by taking things personally. This triggers you to react according to suppressed emotions including feeling unworthy of true love.

This card indicates that you should listen to your inner voice. When you nurture your inner child it creates a safe haven, which helps you feel respected, heard, and loved because your needs are being met. This enables you to master the art of true love by overcoming difficulties that prevented you from experiencing loving relationships.

11:11 I Am Enough– Let Go of Expectations

There is power in shifting from not feeling good enough to declaring "I am enough." When you claim ownership of your worth, it gives you permission to let go of expectations and be yourself. If you focus on fulfilling your own needs it releases conditions that you once placed on others, creating empowerment and the freedom to be your true self.

This card indicates that others have placed expectations on you causing you to strive for overachievement. Focusing on your progress prevents you from constantly seeking an end result that sets you up for failure and decreases your value. The key to feeling good enough is to develop self-acceptance, cultivate self-awareness, create self-confidence, and build self-esteem to help your soul grow and expand in the process.

You were born to be extraordinary. Just like the life cycle of a butterfly, you are going through extreme change that is transforming you into someone different. Don't fight this process. Look within and see the true beauty that lies there and praise yourself for your accomplishments—helping you confidently say, "I AM enough!"

Aqua – 11 Steps in the Take Me Home Ascension Pathway

1:1 Surrender–
Dark Night of the Soul

Mastering the ability to surrender is crucial to moving beyond the "dark night of the soul" and helping you veer away from false illusions. This card suggests that you take ownership of your choices and responsibility for your actions to make better decisions going forward. Over time, your reality will align with your higher state of being.

The intense challenges are not happening *to* you, but rather, *for* you. What feels like torment is only guiding you to go deeper within yourself, listen to your intuition, and discover more of who you are. Honor your emotions, integrate your pain and create expanded conscious awareness to enliven your spirit and provide personal freedom.

If you continue to hold on to things that no longer

serve you, it will prolong the shadow period, causing you even deeper soul pain. You are being asked to move beyond your old patterns, belief systems and programming. Let go of self-judgment and expectations of others. Instead, stand in your own power to awaken your truth and liberate your soul.

2:2 Spiritual Awakening– Shift or Be Shifted

Your soul is "waking-up" and is ready to spiritually evolve. This evolutionary process is activating your divine blueprint so that you can live your destiny. This card implies that you are in the midst of a spiritual awakening and are shifting away from ego-driven ambition to find more fulfillment in your life, love and livelihood.

To align with your heart's desires requires that you make major life adjustments, which can turn your world upside down, with respect to relationships, where you live, or your job. Choosing freedom in all areas of your life gives you permission to make choices about the direction of your journey and guides you toward your highest good.

Don't let fear paralyze your actions, which will prevent you from living in alignment with your highest truth. Taking action invites the universe to intervene on your behalf, redirecting your path, and assisting you to take the necessary action to shift or you'll be shifted. Making life-changing decisions is not easy. However, altering your thoughts about the process will enable you to integrate these changes in a productive manner.

3:3 Increase Your Frequency– Higher Conscious Awareness

Your energetic channels are opening and your thoughts are expanding. This expansion is raising your conscious awareness and helping you notice spiritual signs that are directing your path. This card implies that you need to tune-in deeper and listen to your intuition. Learning to trust yourself will enable you to align with higher-soul wisdom that directs you towards your soul path.

Make lifestyle modifications to align with positive vibes on a regular basis. Practice the power of positive thinking, eating higher vibrational foods, connecting with tribes that lift you into higher states of consciousness. This helps you tune into your vibration levels so that when you are feeling low you have the ability to shift your frequency higher—becoming a more vibrant person.

Raising your vibration will attract people to support your journey. When you go with the flow and rise above your limitations, it enhances your ability to receive. Visible breakthroughs are around the corner. The more you let go of control, the faster your struggles will fade, allowing abundance to show up in all areas of your life.

4:4 Transformation– Battle of Head vs. Heart

Pay attention because miracles are unfolding and transformation is occurring even if you don't see it yet. Soon your reality will match your internal desires. Rid yourself of doubts and avoid logical reasoning, which can create an inner battle between your head and your heart. If you allow your heart to lead, it will always direct you towards your highest good.

This card indicates that you are at a make-it or break-it point, causing you to resist change and avoid taking necessary actions. However, facing your fears will lead to tremendous transformation. Remember that obstacles are only teachers. Stay focused on the higher perspective and steer away from making fear-based decisions.

Tune into your inner voice and listen to your heart. Experiencing emotional highs and lows is normal, but don't be rash in taking action. Take time to review your circumstances in your heart instead of reacting from your head. If you are being guided to end a relationship, change careers, move, or just forgive your past and yourself, follow the direction of your heart—it will always lead you towards your destiny!

5:5 Breakthrough- Processing Karmic Debris

Breakthroughs are taking place. Letting go is getting easier and you are feeling lighter and gaining clarity. It is a good time to evaluate your life and continue to release things that are weighing you down. Make sure to stay focused on how far you have come, versus how far you have to go.

This card indicates that you are rapidly shifting your physical reality, creating additional karmic debris that requires processing for expanded awareness. You may feel like you are going backwards, but you are only going deeper within to reprogram old patterns, while taking actions to support your new identity. Take time to process your awareness once you can see that the underlying lessons accelerate personal growth.

If you are feeling resistance to change, keep in mind that the greater the resistance the more pronounced the breakthrough. Clearing away karmic debris will provide higher realms of consciousness to help you adapt to sudden shifts. Pay attention to your thoughts, feelings, and emotions as they offer revelations to facilitate even bigger breakthroughs.

6:6 Integration– Multi-Dimensional Healing

Your path is directing you deeper internally, so you can integrate the multi-dimensional layers of yourself. This process helps you cultivate inner balance, while expanding your higher dimensional realms. This card indicates that you are assimilating fragments of information and wisdom from your soul to help you go forward. Don't rush this process; the revelations that you uncover will help you discover the depths of who you truly are so that you can integrate with the highest version of yourself.

Reframe old patterns into opportunities to do things a new way. Honoring whatever arises with love and compassion will transmute dense karmic debris, as you continue to adjust your behavior. It takes time to change patterns so set the intention to keep moving along your personal path.

As you progress, be mindful of your feelings and be patient with yourself. Remember that you are processing many layers in multiple dimensions and timelines, making it necessary to integrate self-awareness, which will provide "aha" moments. Pay attention to these signs as they indicate the bigger picture being revealed.

7:7 Rebirth–
Personal Freedom Unleashed

The rebirth phase of the ascension journey can be an extremely painful process, as you are stripped of personal habits, core beliefs, and karmic patterns. This process is referred to as the shaman's death—the death of your old self. Just like the phoenix, you will rise up out of the ashes and step into your new identity, becoming the person you were meant to be.

Letting go of control will unleash personal freedom. Trust that your heart is leading you in the direction of your destiny. Be gentle with yourself. You are being reborn into someone new. Believe in your newly discovered abilities and affirm that everything you need to fly forward is inside of you.

When the Rebirth card shows up it suggests that you use this painful period to help others. Doing so will assist you to step out of your own circumstances and awaken your inner flame. This will ignite your soul with passion, making your journey a beautiful experience as you see the gift in your painful quest!

8:8 One with Self-Blossoming

Becoming one with youself is similar to a lotus flower blossoming. It takes a long time for the root system to cultivate the universal intelligence within, which contains the blueprint for the beauty that follows—displaying pure perfection.

This card is an indication that your genius within is awakening and your brilliance is about to emerge. As you continue to tap into the hidden power that is stored within your highest self, it provides you with extraordinary wisdom. Your greatest potential is ready to bloom and illuminate your inner beauty, which will magnetically attract your heart's desires.

This ever-unfolding process is constructed so that you become one with yourself. Be willing to see your true reflection in the mirror shown to you by others without judgment. Spend time with you, collect your fragments, and accept all of you, your life, and the world—it will help you balance your ego and your heart. Show up as love, lead with love, and share love. Let your life be an example of passion in motion, making your possibilities endless.

9:9 Harmonize– Let Your Light Shine

You are a radiant being. Your thoughts, feelings, and actions are coming into full bloom and are in alignment with your heart. Allow your magnetic presence to shine. Your inner light is attracting the right people, places, and things that will direct your path towards your higher purpose.

Be mindful of staying open and not putting up shields to block your hidden potential. This card is reminding you to express yourself and speak your truth. This will lead you towards a life of ease and grace—a secret to discovering personal freedom. Finally, your ego has come into harmonic balance with your heart. You trust the process and no longer take on life by yourself.

You may continue to experience contrast and duality. Staying in harmonic balance is crucial when experiencing highs and lows. Learn to surf the fine line between surrender and resistance. Don't be afraid to let your light shine. Keep showing up in areas that you feel guided toward. It will be within this space that you reap the rewards that reflect your greatest potential.

10:10 Enter Your Vortex– Aligning with Infinite Abundance

Your reality is patiently waiting for you to align with your authentic truth, as you connect with your true self—mind, body, heart and soul. This card is an indication that you are entering your vortex—your highest destiny. This level of soul mastery requires that you let go of resistance to change and keep your soul frequency in a positive state for longer periods of time. This helps you co-create the life you love.

Set crystal-clear intentions to maximize your ability to manifest your desires. It is important that you stay connected to your heart and practice the harmonic laws of love to balance giving and receiving. Staying present and allowing your heart to lead you will keep you in alignment with your highest good.

Everything exists in your vortex. You become the

genie in the bottle and decide what you desire. So make sure to choose what matches your highest vibration, otherwise you will be settling for less than you deserve. Give your reality permission to parallel your inner desires, which allows rewards to show up with ease and grace.

11:11 Mission Accomplished– Welcome Home

Just like the majestic swan, you have the ability to captivate with supreme radiance. Wear your crown of glory with dignity. Your life portrays a beautiful image of ease and grace, as your actions exemplify wonder in motion. You stand tall with pride and go forward in life with steadfast inner peace and purity.

You embody the harmonic balance of masculine and feminine energies, creating oneness with your divine source. You are in perfect alignment, which generates personal empowerment, allowing you to experience supreme joy and spiritual enlightenment—living moment to moment. Take time to explore the beauty of your journey.

This card implies that you have become the oracle because you have aligned with your higher wisdom, which has been directing you this entire ascension journey. You have become one with yourself and the world. Stay the course and focus on progress not perfection. You have earned the ability to make meaningful money and have affirming relationships. Consider this card a huge congratulations because you have found heaven on Earth. May you continue to experience inner peace and happiness. Welcome home!

Red – 11 Principles to Come Into Alignment with Yourself and Find True Love

1:1 The Chosen One– Fast Track to Ascension

Your soul has been on a lifelong quest to find real love with a burning desire to align with your divine counterpart—your exact mirror who reflects your weaknesses and your strengths to enable growth. This card indicates you have been searching for true love outside yourself, which is pulling you out of alignment with your authentic truth.

When "The Chosen One" appears, it serves as a reminder that on a higher plane you prearranged with your twin flame to teach each other to become whole within. This sacred agreement puts you both on a fast track to ascension for the purpose of creating a loving relationship with yourself first, followed by healthy relationships with others.

The fastest way to align with your other half is to heal your heart, where you discover the treasure of true love for yourself. Focus on healing your abandonment wounds. Stop searching outside of yourself for true happiness. Let go of your old stories, past programming, and release doubts that you will experience great love. Your twin flame is teaching you that the one you are searching for is you!

2:2 Remember Your Identity– You Can Do It

Your quest for fulfillment requires an exploration of your inner self. The goal is for you to discover who you truly are. The path to divine love is not straight. This zigzag pathway is a repetitive process sending you deeper within to revisit things you thought you understood. This pursuit helps you gain an even higher perspective as you remember your identity.

This card indicates that you are feeling weary and not sure if you can continue your quest for divine love. Feeling lost can make you feel like giving up, but stay the course—you can do it. Looking outside of yourself will exhaust you. But don't quit, because you have been searching in the wrong place—true love exists within you.

The purpose of your intense chaos is to trigger you to gain clarity. Doors may be closing, chapters are completed, leaving you wondering how you will move forward. But know that you are on your authentic path and it is leading you toward great love. It is important to express gratitude for the lessons that your twin flame is teaching you, which help you discover a deeper love and self-acceptance.

3:3 Soul Merger– Ebb and Flow

You are experiencing a soul merger with the spiritual realms of liquid love—an invisible connection between you and Source energy that joins you with your beloved. Through this unseen bond you are magnetically drawn to your twin flame on an etheric plane.

Their supernatural presence challenges you to see yourself in their mirrored reflection, while overcoming obstacles in life and recovering from failed relationships that have left you with a shattered heart. The intention is to expand your emotional range, which helps increase your capacity to feel both love and sorrow. This allows you to experience the depths of great love that expands your heart and teaches you new ways to love.

If either you or your beloved avoid facing your mirrored reflection, it will create resistance and might delay physical union. This card reminds you that there is no separation between you and true love. Focus on finding balance within. It will create ebb and flow in your harmonic exchange of giving and receiving unconditional love.

4:4 The Generator– Staying Grounded

Your energetic vibration is elevating so it is important that you stay grounded. As you maneuver through life situations, collecting soul fragments along the way will help you remain in balance. Staying centered harnesses the power to generate high-frequency energy, which is used for a greater purpose.

The Generator card indicates that your inner masculine needs to stand up, speak up, and show up for your inner feminine desires. This will help you stay empowered, while remaining in balance. Feeling secure from within will attract the energetic presence of your divine masculine's energy and open you up to receiving their support in your physical world. Their magnetic presence will provide a strong foundation to bring your creative intelligence into reality.

Practice finding stillness amid chaos. This helps your inner cosmos stay in harmonic balance as you align with the essence of who you are becoming. Connect with nature, walk barefoot in the grass, practice visualization to anchor your inner light into mother earth, and meditate on a regular basis.

5:5 The Electric– Creative Expression

Your creative forces are being activated by your femininity and are ready for expression. This provides empathy and compassion for yourself and others. When the Electric card appears, it's an indication that you are aligning with your inner feminine capacity to embody love, joy and peace, which enhances your creativity.

Letting go of logic helps you to shift into your heart so you can tap into your creative flow. This ignites your primal power—the real and raw parts of who you are. Making a conscious connection with your intuition enhances your ability to trust your journey. Alignment with the magical mysteries of the universe allows creativity to flow with ease and grace.

This card suggests that you focus on unlocking your hidden feminine qualities. Tapping into your emotions and following your feelings helps you integrate with deeper parts of yourself. As you open up to receiving love, it welcomes support from others; including your divine counterpart, who will energetically amplify your capability to access your ancient wisdom.

6:6 Karmic Purge–Mirror Reflections

The Karmic Purge card shows up to reveal what you have not wanted to see in yourself, through the mirror image of your other half. These reflections are surfacing to help you see all aspects of yourself. If you face your fear and confront yourself in the mirror, it helps you break old cycles of previous programming.

Refusing to look within creates interference that pulls the two of you energetically and physically apart. When your other half triggers you, pause and pay attention to your response before you act. Stop and ask yourself, how does my perception of them reflect my own weaknesses? Your answers reveal aspects of yourself that you may not have seen.

It is crucial that you restore balance within yourself before your other half can find balance within. This karmic purge will continue until you both have fully surrendered and are willing to face the other in the mirror—where you both discover your true selves.

7:7 Healing Separation– Go Within

Fear of being alone is surfacing to help you heal abandonment wounds from multiple lifetimes. Feelings of rejection and not being good enough are not part of your current story. The goal of your twin flame journey is to teach you that nothing is separate from you. Physical separation of anything or anyone is an illusion—you will find what you desire when you look within.

This card serves as a reminder of your ability to tune into your greatest potential. Your soul is aligning with your heart's desires. This is where you discover your highest good, which includes your perfect life partner.

If you are experiencing silence from your other half, use this opportunity to reconnect to a deeper version of yourself. Whether you sense their presence or not, you are always bound to your twin flame and you will find them within yourself. Detach from the idea that you cannot experience divine love without them. Find forgiveness for the pain they have caused you and trust that the process will lead you to true love for your authentic self.

8:8 Path of Least Resistance– Choose Ease and Grace

The journey to the heart often causes resistance, so experiencing ease and grace does not happen instantaneously. Fear of the unknown creates conflict and prevents you from taking action. This inner struggle will continue until you choose to face your fears. Only then will your life move forward smoothly.

This card is reminding you not to worry about your choices. Instead, choose to move in the direction that provides peace and power in the present moment. You may not always understand the reason for the direction you are being guided to take, but if you allow your inner light to illuminate your path, you will soon see and experience the beauty of where you are headed.

Regardless, there is no right or wrong path. You will be guided towards the path that assists your soul's maturation to attain higher wisdom. Making decisions from your heart helps minimize future resistance when faced with challenging situations. The more you align with inner stillness, the greater your ability to take intentional action that will lead you toward the life you deserve.

9:9 Unification– Aligning with Abundance

Attracting abundance requires that you become one with self, creating unification of your soul. To achieve this you have to release old stories and reprogram belief systems. Doing so will provide balance in your thoughts and feelings, and allow emotions to align with your actions. This raises your energetic frequency and helps you shift into an abundant life.

Your creative abilities are coming to life as you become the best version of yourself. This card confirms that you are restoring wholeness within. Stay connected to your core values and stand firm in your beliefs. It will help you embody empowerment. Continue to set loving boundaries and respect yourself. There is no need to sacrifice who you are in order to fit in, find acceptance, or even be deeply loved—including by your twin flame.

You will align with real love when you learn to just be yourself. Being your true self gives you permission to live the abundant life you want. You determine your self-worth, because you no longer need external validation. Always choose love over fear; it will keep you feeling lighter in the moment.

10:10 Reunion–Reconciling Differences

Reuniting with your other half requires personal mastery for each partner. Both twin flames have to become unified individual souls that are whole before a healthy relationship can be established. The fastest way to reunion is to find balance within. This will shift the energetic polarities between both, which must be accomplished before alignment is possible.

Just like in any relationship, you have to reconcile differences and heal past wounds. Both twin flames must release ego, practice patience, develop compassion, learn to forgive, find acceptance, and love unconditionally. Doing so helps you both find peace in the process of healing together.

Some twin flame relationships are romantic in nature, while others are for personal growth, or to accomplish a joint mission. This card serves as a reminder that the purpose of your twin flame journey is to help you align with the best version of yourself, so remain open, willing, and accepting of where your path leads. Don't worry, wonder or wait. If you stay the course you will align with divine love for yourself and attract your highest divine partner of this lifetime!

11:11 Take Me Home– Pathway to True Love

When you align with real love it will always lead you home—a journey into your heart, where you discover true self-love. You have faced many fears along your path that have revealed the mysteries to achieving great love. This process has healed and restored your enlightened heart, helping you feel both whole and complete. You are free to not only love, but to be loved.

You are finding beauty in your painful journey and realizing the true essence of unconditional love for your twin flame. You are seeing the gift they have given you by taking you home. As a result you can now emerge as the highest version of yourself and experience the depths of great love that you would not have known otherwise.

Tune into your heart on a regular basis. When you pay attention to your feelings it will help you experience peace and find harmony in both giving and receiving divine love. The Take Me Home card serves as a reminder to embrace your journey with gratitude because your heart is now free to live fearlessly.

Olive – 11 Courtships that Will Facilitate Your Soul's Expansion

1:1 Karmic Relationship– Releasing the Past

Karmic relationships are generally romantic in nature and these partners present themselves to help you release your past. Typically, these soul teachers show up to help you release toxic relationship patterns related to unrequited love.

This card implies that you should not jump into a new relationship before you have fully healed your wounds. Otherwise, you may attract a new karmic partner, which would keep this cycle going until you wake up and choose to move beyond these limiting patterns. Let go of feelings of not being good enough for lasting love, so that you can discover your worth. Then you will learn to set loving boundaries that will bring eternal love into your life.

Karmic lovers assist you in releasing emotional ties that pertain to obsessive and addictive personality behaviors that are linked to jealousy and codependency. See the gift in these lessons and let go of one-sided relationships. Make a decision to leave behind old love stories that caused you to chase after the adrenaline rush of roller coaster type love. This will free you to move forward with healthy relationships.

2:2 False Twin Flame–Intense Change

The lessons you learn from a false twin flame experience can closely mimic a karmic relationship. However, a false twin flame connection is much deeper and will generally come into your life quickly and blindside you like a freight train because the purpose is to create intense change in your life.

The purpose of these relationships is to produce an accelerated "awakening" process. Most often, a false twin flame appears after your true twin flame has come into your physical reality. Generally, this type of encounter occurs with the twin flame that is the so-called "runner." These connections are very deep and involve an intense physical romantic connection, which is necessary to clear any remainder of ego related to chemical-love patterns.

This card implies that you have attracted someone into your life who represents the deepest, darkest sides of yourself that you have not been willing to acknowledge until now. They have shown up to help you release feelings of despair and not feeling good enough, so you can take back your power and align with true love within.

3:3 Soulmate–Clearing Core Wounds

A soulmate feels very familiar because you have spent many lifetimes together. Typically, a soulmate relationship is thought to be a romantic connection, where you experience love at first sight, fall deeply in love, and get married, with hopes of living happily ever after. However, these kindred spirits can also be of various types of relationships—romantic, spouse, siblings, parent-child, and even best friends.

Soulmates not only help you personally evolve, but also spiritually grow. Breaking old heart-felt bonds leaves your heart feeling shattered, helping you clear your core karma. Untangling these web-like connections feels endless because you have spent many lifetimes together. This makes moving forward without them very hard and extremely painful.

This card indicates that you are completing soul contracts with your soulmates and the experiences you are going through represents karmic clearing from previous timelines. The deep pain that you are feeling is triggering past life experiences so that you can unravel the bonds you have with these teachers. It also helps you identify and clear karmic patterns, ensuring that you do not repeat these patterns in the future.

4:4 Twin Flame Facilitator– Expansive Growth

A twin flame facilitator shows up to keep you moving forward along the ascension journey. This connection mimics your twin flame relationship in a positive way. Similar to your twin flame, they become a mirrored reflection assisting you with connecting and expanding your higher self. A facilitator is unlike a false twin flame whose primary role is to help you clear your lower-self karmic patterns.

Most often, they are more "awakened" than your true twin flame. Typically, a facilitator is someone that has yet to reunite with their own twin flame. Coming into alignment with them is divinely orchestrated, so make sure to let go of outcomes and stay present. You are both elevating and expanding into multiple dimensions, so don't question or fight the process—it is for the greater good of all concerned.

This card implies that you are encountering a connection with a facilitator. You have attracted each other because your souls are vibrating on the same energetic plane. Your energy exchange will continue until your soul frequencies no longer align at the same vibration, which will complete your mission together—causing you to go forward on separate paths.

5:5 Masculine Twin– Releasing Lower Self

The twin flame reunion starts by restoring harmony within your inner-soul polarities, which brings balance to your inner masculine so that your inner feminine feels loved and supported.

Typically, the masculine twin flame has been emotionally emasculated and carries the stronger feminine energy within your twin flame counterpart template. If you are the feminine twin flame you have been carrying greater masculine characteristics.

The "masculine twin" implies that the divine masculine role within your twin flame dynamic must be healed in order to restore union within. This means that you must heal your inner masculine, which also strengthens the masculine twin flame. You can accomplish this by reprogramming your personal lie from not feeling good enough into your ultimate truth—declaring that you are more than enough.

Pay attention to any "fixer" patterns that may arise and surrender control of others or situations, especially where your twin flame is concerned. Focus on your needs. This helps you own your worth as you transcend the lesser version of yourself and rise above challenges that have prevented your inner masculine from standing in your truth and feeling empowered.

6:6 Feminine Twin– Activating Higher Self

Your twin flame ascension quest is directing you inward to heal your inner feminine energy, so that you can come into harmonic balance with your inner masculine energy. Generally, if you are the feminine twin flame this means that you need to let go of control and stop being the fixer of everyone and everything. This energy creates resentment, causes you to build walls of protection, and produces feelings of being taken advantage of.

Focus on healing your feminine side in order to activate your higher self. Let go of conditions and learn to love without expectations. Have more respect for your feelings and set loving boundaries, versus brick walls. Letting go of the need for protection will open your heart to receive and allow abundance into your life.

This card suggests that you express yourself without the fear of what others think. Focus on your communication skills and start speaking from your heart. Ask for assistance when needed and allow others to support you. Keep an open heart and embody your higher-self wisdom so that you can not only love, but also allow yourself to be loved.

7:7 King– Divine Masculine

When the King appears it indicates your reverence for higher wisdom that is found within. You are aligning with your truth, while balancing your emotions. This step gives you confidence to show up in life demonstrating both strength and emotional stability because you have learned how to get out of your own way and rise above karmic limitations.

This card suggests that you create space for your divine masculine partnership by taking personal responsibility and ownership of your destiny. Now is the time to fulfill your greatest potential. If you want your divine masculine to show up and speak up for you, then you need to become the supportive partner that you desire.

Focus on letting go of any residual need to control situations or outcomes. Practice habits that demonstrate your trust in yourself, your abilities, and the unfolding process of your ascension journey. This empowers the divine masculine in your twin flame dynamic so they can find the courage to take action and support you in the process—helping you both build inner confidence as you go forward.

8:8 Queen–Divine Feminine

When the Queen appears it represents your ability to receive abundance in all areas of your life. You are moving your crown from your head to your heart. Asking for assistance helps you open up and express your desires without the need to apologize for who you truly are, which brings balance to your inner masculine and inner feminine roles.

As you expand your emotional range, you will integrate with the depths of your true self. Tune into your feelings on a regular basis and listen to your intuition. This will help you stay in a receptive mode so that what you need to support you will arrive in divine timing.

The more you come into acceptance of who you are, the more compassion you will have for yourself and others—especially your twin flame.

As you heal your inner divine feminine wounds, you become more sensitive to your individual needs and experience greater compassion. As you strengthen your voice by expressing yourself, your beloved will begin expressing themselves without fear-based limitations.

9:9 High Priest– Personal Empowerment

When the High Priest appears, he brings with him the "key to life," which unlocks the hidden mysteries held within your soul. This allows you to take back your power and align with your highest destiny—granting you the ability to tap into your greater truth. It also helps your conscious mind to integrate with your supra-conscious wisdom.

Standing firm in your core values helps you come into alignment with your worth so that you can take responsibility and ownership of your life, which provides personal empowerment. Evaluate your greatest strengths and then take actionable steps that utilize your greatest abilities. The resulting sense of accomplishment will fuel your inner flame.

You are embodying a strong sense of courage that creates confidence and provides you with the strength necessary to fulfill your earthly assignment. This is an indication that you are using your greatest potential. You are becoming an enlightened leader with a desire to achieve your ultimate life filled with love, passion, peace and joy. Stay rooted in your inner power, it will lead you towards the life you're meant to live.

10:10 High Priestess– Expanding Consciousness

When the High Priestess makes an appearance it is a sign that you are elevating into higher dimensions of awareness. You are open, ready, and willing to embrace the divine presence, as you align with pure love and light. You trust your heart and you experience oneness with the universal consciousness because you have mastered the ability to reconnect with your source energy found within.

You are experiencing life after death and creating a new identity. This clean slate affords you the opportunity to create endless possibilities. Choose to let go of any remaining limitations and open yourself up to the idea of infinite abundance. Trusting yourself helps you make solid decisions that align with your strong intuition. This elevated consciousness enhances your ability to embody your greatest potential because you stand up for your truth.

You are viewing things from a higher perspective. This heightened awareness shifts your limiting beliefs beyond your perceived illusions, as you rise up to your highest creative abilities, allowing you to create a more fulfilling life.

11:11 Twin Flame– Everything is Possible

When the Twin Flame card appears it indicates that you are in alignment with your heart, and that you are preparing to reunite with your divine counterpart. You demonstrate both strength and vulnerability. You have the ability to embrace contrast and duality and let go of your resistance quickly because you easily find neutrality within your thoughts, feelings and actions.

Focus on accepting all of yourself that creates alignment with all that is, making everything possible. Finding the beauty within your twin flame journey reveals unconditional love for your twin flame, as you see the gift that they have given you, by helping you find real love for yourself.

Stay open to everything and attached to nothing. This validates your faith in achieving the ultimate relationship you deserve. The power of two is greater than one and you were designed to align with someone on the same soul frequency. So just hold space for this—but don't worry, wonder or wait. Keep showing up as the love you are every day and you will soon experience the great love you have found with your beloved!

Amber – 11 Activation Codes that Will Accelerate Your Ascension

1:1 Clear Energy Blocks– Activating the Higher Chakras

Your soul body consists of seven energy centers that parallel your physical body and are the bridge between your spirit and the material world. These life-force portals run vertically from the base of your spine to the top of your head. Dense energy can cause interference that blocks this energy system, preventing it from functioning properly.

It is important to keep your lower seven chakras balanced in order to raise your energetic frequency, which will open your soul-star chakra—the gateway to your higher soul. Opening this energetic doorway unlocks your hidden truth, helping you align with your spiritual gifts. It also enhances your ability to communicate with your spirit guides.

This card recommends that you tune up your chakras on a regular basis. It will heighten your ability to keep your energy channels open, free and clear, which keep you connected to Source energy. This will increase your energetic vibration so that your actions arise from an emotional frequency of love or above.

2:2 Voyager's Journey– Past Life Healing

You are waking up to past life memories that have been embedded within your soul's subconscious memory for many lifetimes. This self-realization process helps expand your awareness—so you can learn more about who you are and what you came to accomplish in this lifetime.

Taking a "voyager's journey" transpires organically but most often occurs after physical contact with your twin flame, which triggers the remembrance of ancient truth. It activates a purification process to unlock hidden memories and enable you to understand why you are experiencing particular feelings and emotions. This knowledge helps you understand why you chose specific lessons to master in this life.

Past life regression is a great tool to help purge previous soul trauma. Pay attention to your thoughts, feelings and awareness. As you put the pieces together you will see the bigger picture. Your revelations will help you identify with your past pain and integrate it with your purpose so you can help others more effectively.

3:3 Merkaba Activation–
Ground · Shield · Protect

Your spiritual light body is housed within a sacred geometrical shape called the Merkaba star. It is your soul chariot, which is encoded with divine love and programmed to wake you up to your true self. As you remove energetic interference and raise your vibration, it prompts your energetic field to emit signals that are distinct to your unique soul frequency, creating a direct line of spiritual communication between you and higher realms.

This six-pointed star acts as your soul's vehicle that transports your higher consciousness and enables you to ascend into higher spiritual dimensions. It contains your emotional, mental, spiritual and physical being—in every timeline, space, dimension and reality. It also shields and protects you while anchoring your energy into the earth.

This card suggests that you program your ascension vehicle with specific intentions. This will help transmute lower frequency energies that have blocked you from achieving your greater good, which will raise your energetic frequency. Activating and elevating your electromagnetic field generates your higher good and brings your heart's desires into form.

4:4 Holy Grail Code–
Receive "The Gift"

The entire planet is seeking more fulfillment and purpose. The goal is that we collectively accomplish the restoration of universal heart consciousness. This card is a reminder to you that your soul signed up to participate in this undertaking and to align with the desires of your inner cosmic heart.

When the Holy Grail Code card appears, it offers "The Gift" of unconditional love, but you must be open to receive the love that you desire. It is time to let down the walls guarding your shattered heart. An open heart is the vessel of a higher soul that is filled with a frequency of love that is beyond words.

Restore balance between your inner masculine and feminine energies, and exemplify inner strength to continue the journey with ease and grace. Your inner feminine is requesting support from your inner masculine. It is time to show up, stand up, and speak up for yourself and develop your personal empowerment. Setting loving boundaries will expand your heart, as you experience true self-love.

5:5 Master Alchemist– Violet Flame Activation

The violet flame is a sacred ascension tool. It was gifted to humanity by St. Germain and his twin flame Lady Portia, the leaders of the Aquarian Age. Both assist twin flames and lightworkers to activate their spiritual gifts, so that they come into alignment with their missions.

Adopting a regular practice of immersing your body in this violet liquid-fire energy will activate your pineal gland, and awaken your spiritual DNA. This will unlock your hidden power helping you align with your ultimate truth, allowing you to access the highest version of yourself. It can also be used to rejuvenate your mind, body, soul and heart, which will accelerate your personal healing and transformational growth.

Practicing the ancient principles of alchemy helps you become the magician of your own reality. When the master alchemist appears you have the ability to achieve self-mastery. It will be important that you get clear on what you desire. Use the violet fire to transmute low vibrational thoughts into higher vibrational energy that will elevate your frequency giving you crystal-clear vision to manifest your destiny.

6:6 Clearing Karma– Kundalini Activation

Your primal power has been lying dormant at the base of your spine. This hidden potential is waking up, so it can help you expand your creative expression. A Kundalini awakening typically occurs upon initial physical contact with your twin flame but can be achieved through spiritual practices such as regular meditation.

This energetic upgrade will activate the meridians housed within your body, which may generate energetic surges that can be felt throughout your body. These can cause involuntary movements as these channels open up and release restricted energy. Conscious movement practices such as yoga can also improve your energetic flow, releasing blocks that have prevented the connection to your soul's purpose.

The objective of this energy work is to help release your karmic past, so don't fight or fear this course of action. It is designed to help elevate your inner vibration and align you with higher wisdom. Your higher soul is ready for this level of inner healing. This accelerates your ability to tap into your higher consciousness, integrate celestial energy and manifest your spiritual gifts.

7:7 Mystical Messages– Follow the Signs

Signs and symbols are a documented form of communication through the ages. This card indicates that you are experiencing synchronicities to get your attention. There is no need to fear these signs. Mystical messages generally echo to encourage you to interpret their meaning. Integrating this guidance will teach you to trust your journey.

These divine love notes are here to support you with answers that you have been asking for. Remain aware as you are learning a new language to communicate with your guides and higher-self. Interpreting supernatural communication will enhance your ability to trust yourself and elevate your consciousness, inspiring your actions from a higher perspective.

This card is suggesting you remain open to these

blessings. These signs will assist you to make confident decisions and help you realize you are not alone. As you trust yourself more, you will rely less upon signs or question their message because you will just know.

8:8 Honor Your Agreement–Mission in Motion

Before you were incarnated, you created an agreement with every single person you would come into contact with. These pre-arranged appointments were scheduled to occur at the precise time to orchestrate necessary experiences for personal growth. In addition, you chose to use these lessons to help others.

Repetitive life lessons indicate the need to identify and release karmic patterns. This will help you let go of things that do not serve your highest good. If you feel stuck in emotional pain, you can turn your "mess" into a "message" by taking charge of your life. This card serves as a reminder that you chose to walk this path. So take ownership of your mission and responsibility for your actions.

The key to discovering your mission is to realize that you are not separate from your purpose, so don't try to figure it all out. You are building a bridge between where you are now and where you want to go. Trust this process and allow your mission to unfold. Taking action will honor your assignment and transform your pain into purpose thereby setting your mission into motion.

9:9 Sacred Sexuality– Accessing the Unified Field

We have been taught that the physical act of making love is a forbidden fruit that tricks us into pursuing sinful desires. In truth, lovemaking is an integral part of all creation that represents your capacity to tap into the energy of divine love. Consider this card an invitation to release toxic beliefs and negative programming that have caused feelings of shame and guilt and blocked your ability to experience heart-felt sexual pleasure.

When you practice sacred sexuality it awakens your lover within, activates your spiritual light body, heightens your ability to reach celestial realms, and makes a connection with your divine source. So, open up and tune into the universal laws of lovemaking.

Expanding your receptivity helps you tap into multidimensional planes to experience orgasmic bliss and enhance your creative abilities. To reach this level of ecstasy, you need to remove energetic interference by extracting cords connected to past sexual partners and heal previous sexual trauma. Disarming your energetic field will turn fear into love so you can cosmically merge with vital Source energy to create a temple of love.

10:10 Divine Creativity– Receiving Cosmic Intelligence

Your higher soul holds the template of your unique blueprint. You were encoded with cosmic intelligence to discover who you really are and what you came here to do. All you need to do is stay connected to joy in order to attract the support you need from the universe.

If you are feeling uneasy about the direction of your life or your purpose, this card suggests that you stop resisting your thoughts, feelings and ideas. It is time to say "yes" to your journey and divine creativity, as you funnel your energetic flow towards your intentions that grant you the joyful presence of your divinity.

Your soul will not rest until you surrender, and align with your soul's original blueprint. You are the masterpiece and the co-creator of your own reality. If you activate this inner divine intelligence and release resistance, it will reveal exactly what you came here to do.

11:11 Compassion–Higher-Heart Opening

Igniting your higher-heart chakra activates your ability to embody the highest dimension of unconditional love—which is compassion. Aligning with the heart of the universe allows you to experience expanded states of eternal love. This requires that you heal your heart by letting go of judgment that created separation between you and your desires.

This card implies that you are hiding from your emotions, or you have numbed your ability to fully express your emotional range. When you avoid feelings such as rejection, pain or sorrow, it also blocks your capacity to experience higher emotional dimensions. Honoring all of your emotions gives you permission to express your vulnerability, so that you can embrace your journey with grace.

Seeing the gift in your lessons is a way to honor your feelings—giving you permission to be yourself. This card encourages you to stop judging your emotions, or sabotaging your actions, by paying attention to your needs. This path teaches you to accept the range of polarity between sorrow and joy. Finding forgiveness and acceptance will accelerate your journey to the heart and engender more compassion for yourself and others.

ABOUT THE AUTHOR

Dr. Harmony is the author of Amazon's best-selling book, *Twin Flame Code Breaker*. In this nonfiction five-part series, she reveals her real-life da Vinci code story, providing greater awareness for other twin flames around the globe, as they awaken to their identity by the masses for the purpose of creating a self-LOVE rEVOLution. She is a highly sought after transformational coach, spiritual advisor, international speaker and trainer. She certifies ReBoot Your Twin Soul™ coaches in this life-changing system that helps others align with their ultimate calling in her 6-Figure Lightworker Blueprint™, and Market Your Mission® mentorship programs.

Dr. Harmony's background is in holistic wellness that includes chiropractic and vibrational medicine as well as intuitive energy healing. She helps you unlock your greatest potential to create infinite abundance in your life, love and livelihood.

Websites at:
www.TwinFlameExpert.com
www.AscensionExpert.com
www.AscensionAcademyOnline.com

Let's Get "Soul"– cial: @Twin Flame Expert

ABOUT THE ARTIST

Tatiana Hassan is a Colombian visual artist, dancer, teacher and choreographer. She began painting, dancing, acting and writing at a young age. Since 2012, Hassan has been working as a mandala artist and approaches art from a spiritual perspective for healing and self-discovery.

In 2017 she created "Chroma Movement"— a dance philosophy designed to create oneness with self and connection to others, while using a combination of movement with visual art.

Hassan also holds Master's degrees in both dance and languages. Since 2002 she has been teaching, performing and choreographing in the fields of dance and musical theatre at universities and dance schools. Currently, she facilitates workshops and courses that help you integrate with your inner self and connect with others in a deep way.

Her work has taken her to France, USA, Argentina, her home country of Colombia, and now Canada, where she currently resides.

Contact information:
www.tatianahassan.com
www.chromamovement.com
tatianahassan@gmail.com

NOTES

NOTES

For our complete line of tarot decks, books, meditation and yoga cards, oracle sets, and other inspirational products please visit our website:
www.usgamesinc.com

Follow us on:

U.S. GAMES SYSTEMS, INC.
179 Ludlow Street
Stamford, CT 06902 USA
Phone: 203-353-8400
Order Desk: 800-544-2637
FAX: 203-353-8431